"OPTIMIZING RUSSIAN LOGISTICS COMPLEX ON FACE OF CHALLENGE"

By
Dr (Er) Om Prakash
Professor
SMS Lucknow

Acknowledgements

All praise to Almighty God for giving me the strength to complete this research.

I would like to express my deepest gratitude to SMS Lucknow Director Prof Bhatnagar

Contents

Chapter 1..3

1.1 Introduction...3

1.2 Title of the research....................................4

1.3 Background.. 4

1.4   6

1.5 Research Objectives................................... 5

1.5.1   7

1.6 Choice of Region (Russia)......................... 6

1.7 Significance of Research.............................7

1.8 Research Structure....................................7

Chapter2.. 8

Literature review... 8

2.1 Russian Logistics..8

2.2 Challenges and opportunities in Logistics.............9

2.3 Conditions and Improvement Potential in Logistics in Russia...11

2.4 Gaps in the literature................................ 12

Chapter 3.. 13

3.1 Methodology... 13

3.2 Research design.. 13

"Optimizing Russian logistics complex on face of challenge"...13

3.3 Research scope..14

3.4 Data collection method...15

3.5 Questionnaire design..16

3.6 Limitation of research..16

3.7 About Company...17

Bibliography..17

Abstract

Russia is a land of vast terrain and huge geographical expanse and so is the potential of Russian Market. As per the World Bank Report, 2014, Russia has immense potential in terms of growth and development on logistics which could touch to the levels of USD 150 Billion mark by 2015. However, Russia holds a 90th rank in the world on the Logistics Performance Index Scale. So this presents an interesting situation, where the immense growth potential exists, but perhaps due to certain conditions, Russia lags way behind. This paper attempts to examine the challenges faced by the Russian Logistics Complex and the opportunities provided by the Russian market. An example company has been considered which is operating very successfully in the Russian market. Based, on the Logistics Processes and operations of the company, existing Literature Review and the exploratory research conducted, some recommendations have also been offered which could help a company to optimize the logistics processes.

Chapter 1.

1.1 Introduction

This chapter of research is intended to provide an introduction of the selected research topic. A brief overview of the background of the study will be given at the starting of the research; afterwards the primary aim of the research and the objectives will be discussed. Finally, the chapter of the study ends up with the scope as well as outline of the research.

1.2 Title of the research

"Optimizing Russian Logistics Complex on Face of Challenge"

As per the World Bank's report of 2014 on "Trade Logistics in Global Economy", based on the survey conducted on over 150 countries, Russia holds a 90th rank in the world on the level of growth and development on logistics. (World Bank Report, 2014). Apart from this, it has low rank in terms of personnel logistics competence, delivery &

International Transport Operations. Russia is a land of vast terrain and huge geographical expanse and therefore the potential of Russian Market in terms of logistics and transport services is immense. It is expected that the growth in the value of these services will touch a USD 150 Billion mark by 2015 (World Bank Report, 2014). This presents an interesting situation where apparently the total market of Russian Logistics business is very high in terms of cost of operations, but the Logistics Performance Index (LPI) is too low, as per the World Bank's report. Although, the growth of operations is almost 15% but the low LPI indicates sub-optimal operating mode of logistics complex. Some studies do indicate this phenomenon, as will be seen in the Literature Review Section, but, this contrast in itself presents an interesting topic of research. The author feels that it is worthwhile to deeply analyse the situation, starting with the research question, a hypothesis, in this context, as presented in the next sections, and carry over the research to determine the reasons of the contrasting behaviour. Hence, the formal research objectives, research questions, a hypothesis and research methodology, compatible with the research topic and to assist coordination of this research will be presented in the subsequent sections.

1.3 Background

From the year 2009, the general downturn in Economy affected the Russian markets in general, but Logistics in particular. The logistics market decreased by 21%, which had a very big effect on the pricing, as the Russian companies started reducing logistic rates to retain customers. The related business, like demand for local transport and warehousing needs reduced to 30% (World Bank Report, 2014). The authors (Graham, 2004) however expressed that the market is very profitable for the companies working in this sector. For one, the huge profit margins had allowed the companies to reduce the price as a resort to the economic downturn. The proper research and revamp in logistic operations can further help to reduce the operational costs. Further, as the economic situation eases, the demand should further increase which can enable the companies to restore their pricing levels and increase profit margins.

Logistics is being regarded as a key business performance parameter by top enterprises, requires new adaptations and improvisations and this has become mandatory for the survival and competitive strategy for the business organization (Graham, 2004). However, the challenges which are observed in the current Russian scenario which comes as a significant barrier is the economic instability, bureaucratic delays and management style differences. (Rushton et al., 2010). Logistics industry in Russia lags far behind Europe and the United States because the Russian transportation resources and infrastructure remain underdeveloped. Nevertheless, the market looks very promising for investors due to development of contract logistics, increasing turnover in the segment of daily demand (convenience) consumer goods, expansion of storage facilities and the introduction of modern IT-solutions).

At the same time, the reports predict that the logistics scenario should improve drastically in the coming years. (RosBusinessConsulting, 2011). The same experts also opine that though logistics is currently experiencing sluggish growth in Russia, but, it has tremendous growth prospects over the next 3-5 years. This sector is still not particularly popular among the Russian companies and providers of logistics services. Therefore, only the large companies currently offer a wide range of logistics services to their clients, again mainly to a few large customers. This scenario will reverse in coming couple of years, resulting in dramatic growth and demand of logistics business. (RosBusinessConsulting, 2011).

Therefore, it appeared to be a perfect sense to choose this sector in Russia, as this provides an opportunity to study the current scenario prevailing in Russia. The author thinks that this is the right period to direct the research in this area as despite huge potential, the market did not rise as much as it should have, post the economic crisis and challenge from 2009 onwards. Thus, the research objectives, research questions, the topic of research itself, research methodology and the efforts have been directed towards the Russian Logistics Complex in the face of the Challenge.

1.4 Research Aims

To study the logistics complex in Russia, determine the existing challenges in improving the quality of logistics, and to recommend the ways to increase the efficiency and optimize the logistics operations.

1.5 Research Objectives

- To *study and* analyse *the logistics complex in Russia*;

- To ascertain what factors can impact the logistics market and pose the challenge in growth of this sector

- To determine the existing

challenges faced by the Russian companies with respect to transport and logistics

- To propose an optimum solution to mitigate the risks posed by these challenges and how the companies can work around to optimize their logistics operations.

These objectives are compatible to the research topic of "OPTIMIZING RUSSIAN LOGISTICS COMPLEX ON FACE OF CHALLENGE". The endeavour would be to analyse the logistics approaches within the company which can have impact on the business performance and profit margins. The current scenarios and the state of affairs in Russian economy although pose challenge to growth and sustain logistics business (World Bank Report, 2014). These challenges pose the risks and impact on the profitability and the business itself, and therefore, the position of Russia with respect to other countries is too low. Therefore, this research aims at recommending certain measures to improve the logistics operations not only to mitigate the risks posed by the challenges but also to bring forth the operational efficiency.

1.5.1 Elaboration of research Objective

As per the expert opinion (RosBusinessConsulting, 2011), in certain areas like domestic markets, logistics has not taken off properly, mainly due to the lack of business to far reaching customers, especially following the economic challenge. Therefore, it is appropriate to conduct a research on the reasons as to why the domestic market did not take off well post the crisis. The research needs to be conducted to ascertain as to why the demand has not reached to the levels, despite the fact that Russia has immense potential.

Some experts have suggested that the recovery of the global and domestic economy is very difficult and will require long time (Rushton et al., 2010). The state of affairs in logistic market is infested with certain lacunae. For instance, the completion of the orders, which implicitly means customers' satisfaction, needs to be achieved in a cost effective way, to maximize the profitability. Logistics business is dependent on many other, for instance, boosting sales with the improvement of customer relationships, and this can be achieved only through satisfied customers, and for which, again logistics play a vital role.

Therefore, with this research, the author intends to ascertain the reasons for these challenges witnessed by the companies, which actually hamper the growth of logistics business. Another challenge, as other authors have highlighted (Prishchepov et al. 2013), are related to the improper management of logistics. Mismanagement in logistics operations might influence the operational efficiency. It is apparent that optimisation of logistics is necessary in order to achieve the required or desired logistics effectiveness since shipping/transportation might be expensive or at least variable (Zhukov 2012). So now the question arises as tohow does one ship or dispatch a the goods from one part of world to another one, while maintaining, the overall optimization and efficiency? This is the key question, even for this research, which needs to be analyzed and ascertained, since logistics are expensive (Stickley et al. 2013) due to the sheer size or weight of the products or the distances which must be covered are extensive in Russian context.

1.6 Choice of Region (Russia)

Based on the analysis of over 150 countries, Russia holds a very low rank in the world in the scale of logistics business. (World Bank Report, 2014). LPI (Logistics Performance Index) reveals that the Russian performance in logistics sector earns them a fairly low rank of 90. The rank has been consistently low especially after the crisis of 2009 which posed a great challenge to the Russian Logistics complex (RosBusinessConsulting, 2011). The country, despite having tremendous potential and the forecast of improvement, surprisingly shows no much sign of recovery, especially in the logistics sector. The potential is such that the forecast for Russian logistics sector for the year 2015 is expected to grow to the tune of about USD 150 Billion mark by 2015 (World Bank Report, 2014). Incidentally, not much prominent research is available as to why the Russian economy is not responding to the new growth opportunities, especially in the logistics sectors. The country seems to lag behind and has consistently earned a low rank. Therefore, the author chose this area for undertaking the research, so as to determine the reasons of lack of the expected growth failing predictions and to possibly offer some useful recommendations to improve logistics performance.

1.7 Significance of Research

The importance and impact of logistics is phenomenal to the organization. For one, it provides the "competitive advantage" – a position of supremacy over the competitors, and makes the company the customers' favourite. (Christopher, 2011). *However, the logistics* industry in Russia lags far behind Europe and the United States because the Russian transportation resources and infrastructure remain underdeveloped. Nevertheless, the market looks very promising for investors due to immense potential in the development in logistics, increasing turnover in the segment of daily demand (convenience) consumer goods and expansion of storage facilities. The research aims to provide a significant appreciation of this potential, and the recommendations on the areas in logistics which would provide maximum returns to the company and help to optimize their operational efficiency.

1.8 Research Structure

The structure of this research is oriented in this manner: The research starts with an introduction giving some background of the topic in first chapter. It follows with the Literature Review in the second chapter. The review dwells on the general corpus of literature available on Logistics in Russia, examining research material available pertaining to this region and reviewing the literature on optimization techniques adopted by some companies to excel in logistics. Third chapter describes the research methodologies which would be used to achieve and fulfil the research objectives and approaches that would be used in arriving at the research findings and recommendations. Chapter four is designated to provide in detail the various logistics models and the ways to arrive at a perfect and optimized logistics model. Finally, the fifth chapter presents findings and results of research in conjunction with the analysed data. Last, but not the least, conclusion of this research presents the extent to which the research objectives have been fulfilled and some recommendations along with some directions for further research.

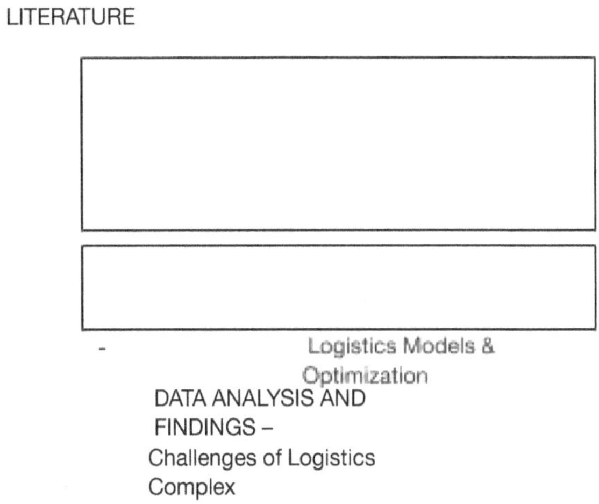

LITERATURE

<table>
<tr><td></td></tr>
<tr><td></td></tr>
</table>

- Logistics Models &
Optimization

DATA ANALYSIS AND
FINDINGS –
Challenges of Logistics
Complex

In the above chapter the research objectives were formulated, relevant to the research topic, along with the explanation and elaboration of the research objectives. The region was also chose as Russia, to conduct the logistics research and the reasons of choosing the company were provided. Also, an illustration in the research structure was given which would act as a research framework to conduct the research.

Chapter2.

Literature review

In this chapter, attempt is made to highlight the deals of the relevant work previously undertaken by various researchers on the topic of study at different times. Following are the specific topics in literature which are examined and reviewed in this section:

1. Russian Logistics set-up
2. Challenges and opportunities in Logistics
3. Conditions and Improvement Potential in Logistics in Russia
4. Gaps in the literature

2.1 Russian Logistics

Sources provide the data (RosBusinessConsulting, 2011) which shows that Russia is one of the topmost countries having the huge amount of expenditures in logistics, which heavily affects rate of goods-production, reduces trades efficiencies, adversely affects healthy competition amongst the companies and affects the country's economy (RosBusinessConsulting, 2011).

Hence, as stated in a research (Armstrong & Associates, 2013), the share of logistics costs in Russia's gross domestic product exceeds a whopping 20 per cent, which is not only the highest among the BRICS (Brazil, Russia, India, China and South Africa) Countries, but is too high even at Global Standards.

Authors (Prishchepov et al. 2013) inform that Logistics is an important aspect because improper management of logistics might influence the profit margins. Therefore, (Prishchepov et al. 2013). It is apparent that optimisation of logistics is necessary in order to achieve the required or desired profit margins since shipping might be expensive (Zhukov 2012). There are many other aspects of the business, for instance, boosting sales with the improvement of customer relationships, which can only be achieved through satisfied customers, and for which, again logistics plays a vital role (Rushton et. al., 2010). In this context, it is interesting to know that some research papers are dedicated much to the study on practical logistics issues that enable the maximization of profit, the minimization of costs and thus the improvement of ROI (Rushton et al., 2010) (Return on investment). These research materials (Rushton et al., 2010) (Zhukov 2012) (Prishchepov et al. 2013) describe in detail the Russian Logistics set-up and are very helpful in the context of the research objectives in the current research.

2.2 Challenges and opportunities in Logistics

Christopher, 2011, informs that importance and impact of logistics is phenomenal to the organization. For one, it can provide a "competitive advantage" – a position of supremacy over the competitors, and make the company the customers' favourite. (Christopher, 2011). In this way, logistics poses a challenge to be competitive, and provide hosts of opportunities if these challenges are meted adequately. A three way relation (Christopher, 2011) exists between the Company, customer and competitor. Customer would always try to seek the advantage, as informs the author (Christopher, 2011). But, the smart company would look at the logistics to reduce its costs, improve the timings of delivery and at the same time try to maximize its profits (Fisenko, 2011). So the author (Fisenko, 2011) clearly identifies that the challenges posed by logistics are reducing costs, improving timings of delivery, satisfying customers and at the same time maximize the profits.

Authors (Zhukov 2012) highlight that winning back customers and improving the customer relations boost sales and profits, so winning back a customer is also a real challenge in Logistics. Therefore, logistics plays a key role in generating the company's revenue and it presents a host of opportunities, if these challenges are meted out appropriately (Zhukov 2012). Thus, converting challenges to opportunities is the key to success in logistics.

One bigger challenge is to effectively plan and control the logistics processes and to manage them internally within the company and coordinate across a huge country like Russia and its various regions (Fisenko, 2011). In this context, the author opines that it is quite essential to accurately forecast the relevant factors, for instance, forecasting cargo-base, understanding and generating multi modal transport-network, forecasting required investment, forecasting production, predicting direction and rate of the science and technical advancement and innovation, and so on (Fisenko, 2011). Hence, the aim for the research should at first be to understand the existing processes of logistics within the selected company, as the Russian area itself is one of the largest in logistics parlance (Armstrong & Associates, 2013). So the understanding and their experience can be taken over, and compared with companies in other regions, within Russia as well as some successful companies globally located. The model adopted by one company can be compared and contrasted with few other successful companies with their model of Logistics (Efimova & Tsenzharik, 2009), and generalize the findings to propose an optimized logistic model of success, leading to business improvement and profitability, especially in Russian context.

To accurately forecast on the parameters, as highlighted above from the research literature, so as to effectively plan and control the logistics processes, one also needs to understand Russia's characteristic shipment strategy in logistics and the available infrastructure. (Posternakova, 2012). Most of the Russian shipment is being undertaken either via rail or through air as there is another substantial challenge in Russian logistics. The roads in Russia have a poor general condition as highlighted from the sources (RosBusinessConsulting, 2011). Train is alternative means of commuting and shipping goods across the country, although it has limited reach-ability compared to Road. But, in many other countries logistics is pursued through land (roads) since this appears to be easier. At the same time this serves as a great opportunity indeed as rail logistics is not so developed in many countries as in Russia (Armstrong & Associates, 2013), so companies can take the advantage of this opportunity. This, in fact helps to serve the biggest challenge facing organisations today, which as per Christopher, 2011, is the need to respond to ever increasing levels of volatility or changes in demand as posed by the customers. (Christopher, 2011)

Some authors have even shown how air logistics can benefit people and businesses (Tuominen, 2009). Russia has developed its approaches due to its size and lack of roads although some countries prefer roads due to ease of operations (ITS Russia, 2013). Furthermore, there are quite a number of roads in countries like UK allowing the logistics companies to ship via land. But, for Russia it is a challenge and a potential opportunity that the logistic diversification provides them to have alternatives to use air/rail/road networks to ship goods which is some times more cost effective (ITS Russia, 2013).

With so much diversity and alternative means of transport and logistics, there are better opportunities to reach out to more customers (Christopher, 2011). But, what is required is to estimate the logistics of optimal reach (Christopher, 2011). This ultimately helps the diversified industries like agricultural industries or software firm which could be set-up easily anywhere (ITS Russia, 2013), even at the vicinity of new sources of raw materials or factors of production, without much worries or botheration of reaching out to their potential customers. Efficient logistics resolve the problem. Therefore, it is important to understand the best ways towards the effectiveness of logistics. Processes need to be improvised, to facilitate long distance service, and capitalize on the efficient modes of movements of goods, in order to make logistics more effective (Christopher, 2011). This provides certain definite advantages of studying the way the model of logistics in the company has excelled, the challenges which were converted to opportunities, which must be analysed and compared with other companies (Efimova & Tsenzharik, 2009). At least this part of the Russian Logistics System, as highlighted in the existing literature, has adapted from innovations and offers efficient and cost-effective solutions (Yug Logistics, 2013).

2.3 Conditions and Improvement Potential in Logistics in Russia

The conditions prevailing in Russia and the improvement potential in logistics can better be understood with reference to a logistics framework *(Christopher, 2011)*. The authors present the integrated logistics complex, its major components, their relationships and operating philosophies in a framework *(Stock et al., 2000)*. This framework seeks to create a single plan for the flow of products and information through a business *(Christopher, 2011)*. The framework is pragmatic in nature and will present performance analysis and improvement suggestions that are helpful to logistics practitioners. *(Stock et al., 2000)*. For instance, in the below diagram the author highlights the typical logistics activities required at each stage of production:

(KORECKÝ, 2012)

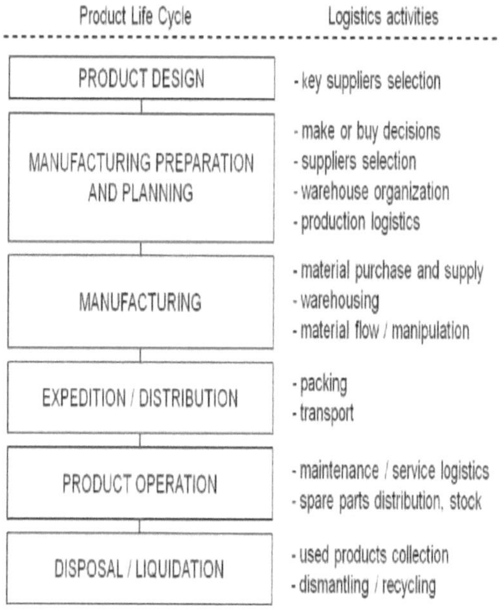

Source: Product life cycle and its relation to logistics activities (KORECKÝ, 2012)

The authors inform that in a Product based company from the first stage to the last stage of production, for instance, the importance of logistics is substantial. Thus, from the stage of product design, where the corresponding logistics activity is to select the suppliers, to final distribution, where the corresponding logistic activity is Transport, the logistics activity is present at each stage and closely coupled with each production phase. As per the author (KORECKÝ, 2012), it is important to understand the logistic framework, in conjunction with each stage of production so that one can appreciate the conditions of the logistics complex. The author further states that there is a factor of risk involved at each logistic stage, which can affect the corresponding stage of production. For instance, if the supplier selection is wrongly made, it can severely affect the production (KORECKÝ, 2012). So there is risk involved and it is necessary to address the risk by coming up with a relevant risk mitigation plan.

The author further suggests that the risk management has become the integral part of logistics management as it helps in improving the conditions of logistics (KORECKÝ, 2012). The risk management in logistics follow the standard procedures. The logistics of industrial enterprise (Fisenko, 2011) includes especially all the activities (KORECKÝ, 2012) pertaining to material flow in company (Christopher, 2011). These activities include material inflow (Fisenko, 2011) from suppliers, warehousing, and material flow in production packing of goods (KORECKÝ, 2012), expedition and distribution to suppliers (Christopher, 2011). It also contains the transport of material (Christopher, 2011) and goods during above mentioned activities (Fisenko, 2011). Logistics can be understood as the way of management of these activities (Christopher, 2011) that contributes substantially to the efficiency of the enterprise (KORECKÝ, 2012). The proper logistics management can reduce cost (Fisenko, 2011) in supply chain, manipulation of material, (KORECKÝ, 2012) cost of warehousing. The production logistics can shorten the lead time in production. It means that besides shorter delivery time of products (Christopher, 2011) which helps the company to be more successful in winning orders it also decreases the volume of material and work in progress that decreases the necessary financing of the company (Fisenko, 2011). Generally the logistics is able to contribute to the company competitiveness mainly by reduction in time (Fisenko, 2011) to deliver the products as well as the reduction of their cost.

2.4 References to Optimizing Logistics in Literature

Logistics permeates all functions and departments of the enterprise for the purpose of optimizing a stream for materials, information and financial flows (Aastrup 2003). The author (Aastrup 2003) further opines that the logistics necessitates a considerable amount of strategic planning and requires a lot of pondering in order to channelize new resources in optimizing their operations. The crux and the critical approach here is to achieve the optimization in strategic areas. The ultimate approach is towards the optimization of all processes related to the organization of production in order to achieve their goals (Khajavi et al. 2014). But, in the research context, and within the context of selected region and company, it is important to appreciate the ways in which the logistics parameters could be optimised in order to improve the profit margins of the business. In this research context, there is not much evidence of previous research that European logistics companies are aware of shipping big machinery goods via rail permitting people to use the motorways without disruptions.

Some companies need to revamp their logistics management, improve services and reduce costs, and for this they must acquire awareness of the many different facets of logistics and the supply chain. As the researchers Rushton et. al. (2010) suggest that they may still not be very clear as to how to manage their logistics in best possible way, and hence they could experience reduction in profits or even incur some financial losses due to this lack of understanding or sub-optimal way of operating (Rushton *et al.*, 2010).Due to good conditions of the roads, the authors (Rushton *et al.*, 2010) say that it has become customary or a culture that, for instance, European companies tend to use roads as a primary means of transport in supply-chain network, despite the fact that road transport is the costliest affair. In Russia, however, the conditions of roads are poor, in general. At times Train is the cheapest mode of transport and there is one added advantage to it (Rushton *et al.*, 2010) as it is less risky. But, there are other factors as well in the transport systems, which lend a fair degree of complexity to the logistics ant its optimization. The cost calculation is not as direct and apparent as it may appear (Rushton *et al.*, 2010), but, it involves a considerable amount of research, analyses, estimations, forecast and recommendations. Some researchers (TSENG *et al.*, 2005) suggest that even though the recommendations have been made, and the company starts operating optimally, but, the system must again be re-evaluated every five years at least or at some other ideal frequency (TSENG *et al.*, 2005). This is the reason that the research on logistic topics is necessary (TSENG *et al.*, 2005). It is possible that in some cases the road transport is cheaper for some companies at some regions, but mostly it is observed that the motorways could be shut during transportation of big goods and the traffic is slowed down and congested whereas rail shipping does not cause any such problems (Rushton *et al.*, 2010). Therefore, it is essential to advance current state of the knowledge in logistics and it is recommendable to introduce an effective option for rail opportunities, and this aspect is worth analyzing. Thus, as it was highlighted a novel approach is intended to be developed in this thesis to give an insight into the optimisation of the logistics processes

(Rushton *et al.*, 2010).

A company can be successful only on the basis of system optimisation of the complex software processes and other production as well as marketing techniques, which all form the basis of modern logistic processes within the organisation of movement of material and information flows(Liao & Kao 2014). Such attributes as marketing techniques, relationships with suppliers and relationship with customers are believed to have impact of logistics and the quality of production (Liao & Kao 2014). It will be discussed how to optimise and improve these aspects to achieve better logistics solutions. One is aware that most operations, techniques, processes, customer relations, logistics management, supply channels, and host of attributes are different for each business, and no matter how similar the product or service line of two companies seem equivalent, but, there are a lot of factors and parameters which can make a world of difference . Therefore, some of the companies are successful, like the example company "X"[1] (X International Transport Ltd, 2014) but many European or Russian failed to survive and succumbed to the load of logistics. So the company "X", which is flourishing should be researched and the resulting findings an:d analyses could be further presented and the model of success proposed along with their approach . This model and experience can then be considered to be applied to other similar companies.

Lastly, in this section, it would not be inappropriate to express the significance of people management, and their relationship which is of paramount importance, since the business can depend on supplier relationships and it is always human resource management which matters to some extent (Wagner & Sutter

---

[1] While conducting the interviews and survey for this Logistics company, the company's executives requested to keep the confidentiality by camouflaging the name of the company and presenting all the information anonymously.2012).. The objective in this research will also be to analyze the impact of human relationship between the contractors, suppliers and consumers with the company and to evaluate their significance (Wagner & Sutter 2012).

2.5 Gaps in the literature

Despite advanced research topics and material

are available for the review, but, the author could not search or verify the optimization techniques, exactly use to optimize the logistics processes. Not many papers highlight the exact procedure, program and plan to reduce total cost of operations and optimize the logistics process. Even if some basic procedure to optimize is given, but, a major corpus of literature, academic articles, journals and research theses do not provide enough matter on comparison of two or more companies.

In the Literature Review Chapter, latest corpus of literature and several academic papers were reviewed pertaining to the Russian Logistics. In the Russian context, several challenges and opportunities as see through this literature were highlighted. The ways the companies optimized their processes, either to increase customer satisfaction or raise their profitability, in the face of challenges, were also reviewed. Finally, some gaps were noticed and were highlighted and it is expected that this research will add-on to the existing corpus of literature and add value.

Chapter 3.

3.1 Methodology

This chapter consists of the overall methodology that will be used to conduct the research. Methodology comprises of all the activities that are required to conduct the study and generate it into a report.

The new knowledge is proposed to be developed which follows the objective of the research using the research methodology in a systematic way and offer the recommendations. There are certain well defined steps that are proposed to be followed in a sequential manner to achieve the final answer to the research aim. The research purpose, methods and strategy of the research have already been introduced earlier and will be explained in this chapter in the context of research methodology.

3.2 Research design

Research design is a blueprint or a detailed plan for how a research study is to be completed. Based on the purpose of research, researches can be classified into four categories (Collis & Hussey, 2003) -- Exploratory Research, Descriptive Research, Analytical Research and Predictive Research. As it was already stated that the current research is more on the qualitative side, so the current research is exploratory in nature. The research topic is already formed and formally the topic is reiterated as under:

"Optimizing Russian logistics complex on face of challenge"

The research objectives have also been stated clearly and this research would attempt to answer and fulfill the objectives of the research. The research process will be iterative in nature and in each iteration (Saunders *et al.*, 2007) the newly acquired learning would reflect on the research ideas continually, and the research and the methodologies could be tweaked as required. Some of the research sections can also be revised at some stage if felt appropriate and it is during the final or concluding stages of the research that one can expect the final version of research findings and recommendations. The iterative research process to be followed is represented as hereunder:

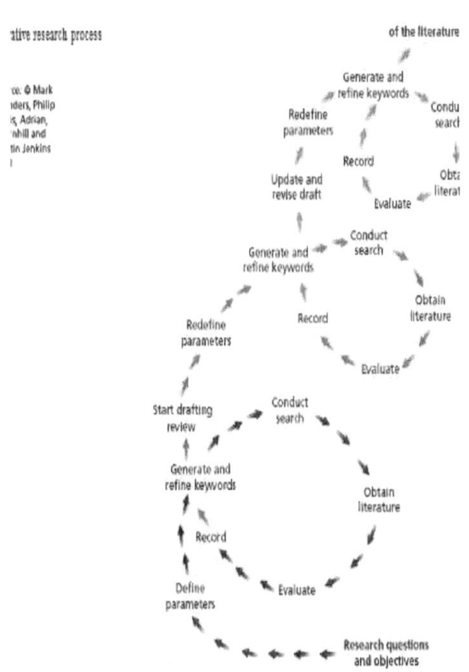

Source: Iterative Research Process
(Saunders *et al.*, 2007)

In this research design process, the data collection is required, in the way as described and accomplished in the next sections, for the qualitative and quantitative research perspective. This research is pretty much qualitative, as already stated above, and the researcher has collected the primary data as a result of interviews, questionnaires, surveys and the first hand reports and documents from the company called "X" International Transport Ltd (X International Transport Ltd, 2014) .

3.3 Research scope

The scope of this project is to research on the Russian logistics services employed in logistics and to propose an optimisation of the overall logistics process. The logistics companies which have been historically using roads as the logistics means; however, the European Union is expanding towards post- Soviet countries where rail was more preferred than logistics. There are drawbacks of roads due to their general conditions in Russia which considerably affects the Logistics efficacy as it renders a fair degree of uncertainty. Therefore, in this research, various Logistics alternatives will be considered, compared and contrasted in Russian context.

A European/Russian company called "X" International Transport Ltd. (X International Transport Ltd, 2014), which is one of the foremost Logistics Company in the area and beyond, would be considered and analyzed to serve the research objectives and miscellaneous other purposes, as would be required in this report. Various questionnaires, survey questions and interviews have been designed and directed towards the company to collect the firsthand data which will qualify as a primary resource (Saunders *et al.*, 2007). The researcher has also spoken with various executives of the company and has sought their permission to participate in the surveys and interviews. The questionnaires and interview transcripts will be attached at the Appendix.

Comparisons of the analyses, results and findings from the primary data collected from (X International Transport Ltd, 2014) International Transport Ltd., with other companies would be in-scope of this research. Similarly, those regions from where the products or services are imported from the other countries to Russia in logistics perspective would be in-scope of this research. The products or services which are exported from Russia to other companies would also be in-scope of this research.

Collection of the data, analyses, results and findings which could qualify as the primary data from the companies other than "X" International Transport Ltd. (X International Transport Ltd, 2014), will not be in- scope of this research. Also, those regions from where the products or services are not imported to Russia in logistics perspective would be out of scope of this research. Similarly, those regions where the products or services are not exported from Russia would be out of scope of this research.

The researcher adopts the research process and design from the "Onion" (Saunders *et al.*, 2007) of research which displays several layers, wherein the peripheral layer is the overall research methodology a researcher will adopt. The research philosophy of Interpretivism was highlighted and the researcher adopts this as initial layer. The research is more on qualitative and inductive approach, and the remaining layers would be compatible with this approach. So as the researcher peels another layer of the "onion", the analysis and data collection would require the adoption of compatible strategy (Johnson and Clark 2006). The use of qualitative methods in the form of case studies would be used to create an in-depth and rich account (Yin 2003;Scholz and Tietje 2002; Rubin and Rubin 1995) of how the company has employed the efficient and cost effective logistics strategy and deployed best possible Supply Chain Network, where many companies in the same area of operations have failed to generate even a fair amount of profitability.

3.4 Data collection method

In logistics domain, there are many circumstances which entail the use of qualitative research interviews. Some of these situations are as follows (Saunders *et al.*, 2007):

- the purpose of the research – which is exploratory
- the necessity and the significance of establishing personal contact;
- the nature of the data collection questions which are complex and open-ended
- length of time required and completeness of the process is long as logistics is a complex process

Therefore, the data collection questionnaires

and surveys are prepared in the context of qualitative analysis and design of the research. It is necessary to take a prior consent from the company's executives for their participation in the surveys and questionnaires. The primary data constitutes the actual interview transcripts, survey responses and participations and the firsthand reports and information generated by the company which could be used in support of the interview and survey responses.

3.5 Questionnaire design

A survey and interview questionnaire design is based on the qualitative research perspective. Mainly, the principles in designing the questionnaire were based on the nature of the data collection questions which is both complex and open-ended. The length of time required and completeness of the process is long, so the questionnaire, response, survey and its response has a scope which requires a longer time-frame of collection. The research questionnaires are attached at the appendix. An attempt is made to attach the transcripts of interview responses as well as the survey responses, after getting a due consent of the participants.

3.6 Limitation of research

The model developed for collection of the data has some limitations due to the fact that some executives, although consented, but could not give proper time for the interview and responded through emails. So there may be some discrepancy between the response and the actual process, operations and data. These limits, however, may not have a major effect on the overall research process and authenticity of results but there could be some influence on the input of values. The data in this study consists of 12 months so although the findings may not be perfectly accurate, but, researcher feels that it can still provide a reasonable degree of accuracy. Further normalization and standardization of the data may be required by either collecting some more primary data or with the help of applying secondary data to the overall model.

3.7 About Company

"X" International Transport specialises in delivering all types of cargo to Russia (X International Transport

Ltd, 2014). This company has been selected due to the following reasons:

- It has rich experience of industry and Russian knowledge the company is capable of assisting in a variety of logistics requirements.

- The staff is based out of Moscow and the UK. The staffs have the bilingual skills in English and Russian and possess several years of experience under their belts in the

Russian freight environment.

- The company's clients are a variegated mix of multinational companies, interior designers, event management companies, individuals and a couple of "oligarchs". Oligarch is a member of an oligarchy or someone who is part of a small group that runs a country; A very rich person (especially in Russia). The company maintains to provide the "Brilliant service" – all confirmed by their customers as being delivered promptly and without any issues.

- The company is one of the most major companies with its operations in Europe & Russia. It undertakes logistics assignments to ship across the country and outside of Russia. The shipping costs are quite high due to the distance and remote places.

Russian Federation is the biggest country in the world and it is lacking in roads in some areas however it is known that the Russian rail network is good, almost comparable to American rail networks (Rushton *et al.*, 2010). It is apparent that is it probably impractical to ship heavy goods via air because those could be massive in size and heavy in weight. However, heavy goods can be shipped via rail using freight carriages. The company uses many ways to transport, from the Trans-Siberian rail, to roadways and shipping as the means of transport in their logistics, and a detailed study would further reveal clear understanding of their logistics strategies and the transportation efficiencies.

The vast majority of entrepreneurs sooner or later face important challenges such as the delivery of goods to the consumer. Historically, the share of rail transport in the Russian Federation was more than forty percent of all freight (Cai et al. 2013). In addition, certain categories of goods can be delivered exclusively by rail in many regions of the country (Aastrup 2003).

With all the obvious advantages the delivery of goods by rail has a number of features. Similarly, shipping by roads or through Air has advantages of sorts. Understanding of all the nuances of this is quite difficult and requires good understanding of logistics optimization. The ignorance of basic rules and norms entails a consequence, costs, moral and financial losses. Optimizing all processes as to how to organize the international or domestic transport in best possible manner is the logistics strategy within the company. The company (X International Transport Ltd, 2014) follows that the Logistics is the science of monitoring, planning and management of transportation, storage of goods such as raw materials, their processing and delivery of the final product to the consumer. Besides material things, as the company maintains (X International Transport Ltd, 2014), logistics is engaged in storage, transmission and processing of information on these shipments.

The company's transport logistics connects all parts of the transportation process into a single chain such as selection of the optimal route, or several types of transport (multimodal transport), preparation of necessary documents (including customs), the organization of loading and unloading and other logistics company takes over the functions of single operator responsible for the entire transportation process from design to unloading at destination. On request, the company (X International Transport Ltd, 2014) organizes cargo insurance, warehousing services, security services, registration at customs, etc.

In this chapter 3 above, which mainly pertains to

the research design and methodologies adopted to conduct the research, an example company was identified, which would be ideal for conducting such research. However, it was also highlighted that due to explicit request from the executives of the company, the name of the company was camouflaged, to maintain anonymity. However, the precise details of the methodology to be adopted, research design, surveys and questionnaires design and the way the analyses would be done was clearly mentioned.

Chapter 4.

The significance and approach of logistics as adopted by "X" Company will be discussed in this chapter in the context of the research objectives. It is apparent that large logistics enterprises use a special approach for meeting their goals and succeeding in their Logistics management decisions (Roh et al. 2014) in the face of stiff challenges as offered by current state-of-affairs in Logistics.

4.1 Russian Logistics Complex in the context of "X"

In accordance with the research objective, it would be vital and crucial to consider the logistics complex for a large enterprise like "X". In researcher's opinion it is crucial to look into the problems and challenges as given below and try to understand and recommend to further optimize the efficiency of the operation, if possible. This is to attempt to make some reasonable grounds for the next level of development of transport and logistics complex 'TLCx' in Russia. The most important part in the so called 'logistics complex' approach is to provision the resources, providing them for the whole nation-wide transport systems, especially in establishment and operability of railways, roadways and other networks, like airways, sea-going and river- ways and their corresponding infrastructure.

The Object and necessities for a logistics organization, like "X", for undertaking the resources provisioning

for the whole transportation sector could be

associated with the following factors:

a. There is a need to undertake a consolidated and integrated logistics approach which synthesizes the methodologies (Fisenko, 2011) of general system theory, Information technology, systems engineering, cybernetics, marketing, management and other disciplines. (X International Transport Ltd, 2014) This allows solving the challenges of movement of goods and information flow from their places of origin to the place of destination.

b. Second factor is that the logistics helps to create those conditions which assist in removing the most acute conflicts and challenges (Fisenko, 2011) faced in between different segments and activities in the transport sector as it implies a potentially high harmonization or matching of the economic interests of all participants in supply chains, complexes and systems. This in turn helps o mitigate the risks posed by these challenges and how the companies can work around to optimize their logistics operations.

c. Another factor is that the logistics offers

very powerful resource saving potential as the big organization can adopt a very systematic approach to manage and optimize not only the materials flow but also other economic and information flows during the operation, construction, reconstruction, repair and maintenance (Fisenko, 2011) of transport networks. This resource optimization helps in optimizing the logistics processes to a large extent, thereby enabling the companies to improve their efficiencies and cost effectiveness.

For the effective planning, organizing and coordinating the logistics processes across the country like Russia and its sectors of the economy, very accurate forecast is necessary. For instance, forecasting the resources, forecast of the cargo-base, (Fisenko, 2011) predicting the development of multi-modal transport network, forecasting of the investment, predicting the plausible industrial production, anticipating directions and rates of the scientific and technological progress and innovations, etc are required. These forecasts give opportunity to (Fisenko, 2011) predict in advance, to plan and allocate resources in order to meet new challenges instead of implementing expensive changes in capacities boot redistribution process and use of reserves. This helps in achieving the final object of mitigating the risks as posed by these challenges.

4.2 Operating Variables of logistics

For a company like "X", in the context of Russian region, there are mainly five main variables of logistics at any, or most, enterprise levels. First these variable would be discussed and then the method of operationalizing those variables. These variables would finally help in recommending an optimized solution to the logistics complex. These variables are as follows (Fisenko, 2011):

a. Purchasing
b. Production
c. Distribution
d. Transportation and
e. Information.

To undertake any logistics activity a company (buyer) must be found or should exist who would be willing to purchase some product. The whole business of logistics actually is built upon supplying the product or services to the buyer or purchaser of such product or services. The there are Suppliers who may have various raw materials or semi-finished products (Wagner & Sutter 2012); hence production needs must be considered where the raw materials can be alternatively purchased from the various suppliers. To optimize the process of procurement of raw materials, the logistics complex must be aware of these alternative suppliers. So whether it is for Supplier or buyer, delivering products is the key in logistics (Wagner & Sutter 2012). Thus the enterprise must focus over the distribution.

Logically speaking, various transportation means (Aastrup 2003) must also be considered when delivery (Wagner & Sutter 2012) is concerned. Company may use national or private transportation services. A good logistics process would compare and contrast the various available transportation services to which the company can outsource the delivery. However, some companies have their own logistics departments and they perform their own transportation services. Information has always been the key in any matter (Aastrup 2003). Notwithstanding, the companies would keep all the information to deliver the products by optimal means of transportation. Thus, some companies may have the capability to send the products through the truck-trailers, but, at the same time for a country like Russia, sending the goods through rail may be more advisable. The largest companies like "X" also consider rail as their important means in their arrangement of logistics. Therefore, this can be a learning process for many other companies wish to optimize and reduce the costs of transportation. Information is therefore the key to optimization in this context.

Thus, within the large logistics enterprise, there are several operational variables that need to be considered. One of the biggest considerations is the 'Logistics outsourcing'. For the companies like "X", it is the most vital and crucial consideration for planning their strategy for logistics as their involvement in Rail transport or even Airways usage means a clear need to outsource. Within the Outsourcing itself, there are several other operational variables or fields (RosBusinessConsulting, 2011) which need to be considered. Basically, there are 4 other operational fields the companies must consider:

a. Transportation – as has already been highlighted

b. Freight Forwarding

c. Warehousing

d. Logistics Management

These operational variables or fields are used to optimize the logistics processes by the company to resolve the challenges as posed by Logistics complex, which include customer satisfaction and timely delivery (RosBusinessConsulting, 2011). Transportation was already discussed earlier. Sometimes the companies need to export their products or import the raw materials from other companies. At that time the concept of freight forwarding is used and this relieves the formidable task of negotiating multiple carriers, costs and modes involved to deliver a product from say a place in Russia to a destination in some other country. A more detailed discussion on the variables follows in the next section.

4.3 Major Components for Optimization

For a company like "X" (X International Transport Ltd, 2014), transportation is the major component in the logistics arrangement. Transporting products across the country naturally involves major challenge in terms of cost and involvement. This is the most important field and major focus must be given on optimizing this field (RosBusinessConsulting, 2011). Related to this field is the need of warehousing services and it accounts for the time between the manufacturing and actual shipping of the manufactured products (RosBusinessConsulting, 2011). Similarly there is impact on the costs accordingly as well.

Hence the actual transportation is the major component of the Total Costs of Operations (TOC) in logistics. Freight and Warehousing are the next significant fields (RosBusinessConsulting, 2011) and they involve such activities as cost of lease of storage space in commercial use, operating expenses and cost of safekeeping services. Safekeeping accounts for the safeguarding of the product from the time of dispatch to the time of final delivery (Wagner & Sutter 2012) to the buyer. It may also include insurance costs which covers the risks of damages in transit.

The major aspect of interest in this research comes from the fact that there is a fair degree of competition in the Russian transport and logistics services (RosBusinessConsulting, 2011). This provides a major challenge to the Russian Logistics complex. To resolve this challenge, the company like "X" takes the help of the key players -- the third party services segment which is from the providers and top players from the western logistics companies (National Credit Bureau, 2010). These companies have extensive experience in providing the services especially to the majority of manufacturing and product companies across the global. So huge companies like "X" resolve the challenge by outsourcing some of their activities to these companies. It is understood that their extent of servicing and operations globally as well as in the Russian market is based on the activities, growth and number of business transactions of their main customer in Russia, for instance the "X" company itself. As per the measured estimates from the data of companies retrieved from the National Credit Bureau, the revenues of TOP transportation and logistics companies account for billion dollar roubles. (National Credit Bureau,

2010). The main reason for outsourcing is to resolve the challenge of competition by optimizing their processes. Therefore, it means that they undertake outsourcing for optimization (X International Transport Ltd, 2014). Thus, outsourcing is the other key to successfully optimizing the logistic process and the companies which need to save their cost of logistics operations, may consider this way of optimizing their processes.

4.4 Outsourcing for Optimization in the face of challenges like competition and profitability

So, it is clear that the Logistic Outsourcing is the major factor which brings the competitive edge to the manufacturing enterprise utilizing their services (X International Transport Ltd, 2014). This is the reason that a proper weight must be assigned to this field or variable to optimize the logistics costs. Some companies out-source the activities after proper analyses to reduce the costs. Economies of scale help to reduce the costs (Fisenko, 2011) in total operations. 3PL companies have large scale volume in business transactions of identical activities. For instance, their role could be just to facilitate the transfer (Fisenko, 2011) of heavy goods through rail from Place A to Place B. The bulk transactions help them to optimize their operations, and therefore costs (Fisenko, 2011), and carry forward this saving to their client, so as to be competitive in their own category of 3PL providers. In this way, a smart manufacturing enterprise like "X" (X International Transport Ltd, 2014) seeks this opportunity to reduce its own Total cost of Operations (TCO) as for them also the major component in costs is transportation. This also came out evidently form the primary resources and the surveys and interviews conducted. The object of this paper as highlighted above was to recommend the best ways of optimization of logistics in the face of the challenge. Following the model of the company "X", much of the costs in logistics can be saved in this manner, by following their model.

Thus, we see that how the various factors help in reducing the costs and whilst some companies increase the margin of their profits, others carry forward their savings to customers, as Sales price is one of the decisive parameters affecting the Sales. Profitability is another challenge (Fisenko, 2011), which is also dependent on many other aspects of the business, for instance, boosting sales with the improvement of customer relationships, and this can be achieved only through satisfied customers, and for which, again logistics play a vital role. Rushton et. al. (2010) dedicate much of their study on practical logistics issues that enable the maximization of profit, the minimization of costs and thus the improvement of ROI (Rushton *et al.*, 2010) (Return on investment).

So, in the face of challenges like competition and profitability, logistics has an important role to play as improper management of logistics might influence the profit margins (Prishchepov et al. 2013). It is apparent that optimisation of logistics is necessary in order to achieve the required or desired profit margins since shipping might be expensive (Zhukov 2012). So now one question arises, and which must be optimally answered and it was posted in the survey, that how does one ship or dispatch a trailer or goods from one part of world to another one, while maintaining, or even maximizing, the profit margins? This is the key question, for this research, which had to be analyzed and ascertained, since logistics are expensive (Stickley et al. 2013)due to the sheer size or weight of the products or the distances which must be covered are extensive. In the context of Russia, which is the largest country in the world, the analysis of this question is of paramount importance. While analysing this question, it was ascertained that the information was the key to decide on the particular consignments and orders. Wherever feasible, the company used the Rail networks, for instance, for long-haul deliveries as the conditions of the roads are poor. The cost and reputation risks involved are huge and sometimes irreparable as came out from the analyses of the primary resources. In some cases Rail transports acted as reliable and economical modes of transport. Thus, it is seen that the importance and impact of logistics is phenomenal to the organization. For one, it provides the "competitive advantage" – a positional of supremacy over the competitors, and makes the company the customers' favourite. This phenomenon is explained by the researcher in a 3-way relationship. (Christopher, 2011) The 3-way relation exists between the Company, customer and competitor. Customer would always try to seek the advantage, as informs the author (Christopher, 2011). But, the smart company would look at the logistics to reduce its costs, improve the timings of delivery and at the same time try to maximize its profits. For instance, as it was seen that company "X" would apply its best information resources to arrive at the optimal route in a particular case of the logistics in a cetain consignment delivery.

Significance of supply chain on the logistics of the manufacturing enterprise is also one factor which merits the mention in this chapter and worth its consideration with respect to research object of optimizing the logistics function. The role of Supplier in delivering the raw materials was already highlighted. While in the previous section we considered the effect of the variables and their operationalization for the purpose of research analysis, here we undertake some exploratory research and quality of some suppliers and the modes they operate, which can have a bearing on the overall logistics strategy for the manufacturing enterprise. The two functions of logistics and supply chain are quite interconnected as described earlier, especially for the manufacturing enterprise, and the impacts are received from the customer focus and information technology--the key parameters in logistics. The management function in logistics integration and supply Network coordination has its bearing on Supplier and Buyer performance and reaction (Chen and Paulraj, 2004), as it has an impact on costs. Customer Focus and Buyer's reaction in turn has the bearing on the optimization of the logistics function and this works pretty much as a chain (Chen and Paulraj, 2004) as all these factors are inter-related. Thus, this is an interrelated phenomenon and lends a fair degree of complexity and its delineation is an object of research.

Smart organizations take this as a challenge and after careful analyses and study, optimize this whole cycle by changing that aspect which adds more value. For instance, some organizations would take the help of information technology to automate this process itself and there are various solutions and models of IT Software in Logistics and supply chain (Chen and Paulraj, 2004). One example of such software is Oracle's Logistics and Supply chain Management Solution.

The theoretical foundation which has been

provided here is fairly comprehensive and has many facets and should definitely assist in reaching the goal of competitiveness (Chen and Paulraj, 2004) .This would definitely assist in creating and evaluating the proposed research model as envisaged. Whilst this illustration of theoretical foundation of Internal Logistics opens new vistas to the subject, it also highlights the importance of optimized external factors, and thereby the internal logistics within the enterprise (Chen and Paulraj, 2004). The consequent outcome results in the creation of the proposed research model which is so comprehensive that it should ultimately help in rendering logistics process optimization. As many companies to do hold their key information resource, it is also propose to use software to enter the parameters of the model and evaluate the model with the various inputs and variables as discussed so far. This is another key recommendation from this paper and it clearly serves one of the object of this paper – to optimize the logistics complex and mitigate the risks in the face of the afore mentioned challenges.

4.5 Significance of Various modes of Transport in Russian Logistics complex

Significance of Railways and Roadways on Russian logistics complex is remarkable and so are the associated challenges, risks and various risk mitigation strategies as discussed and researched (Takata & Yamanaka 2013). In this category of rail-road transport, there is a significant contribution of 3PLs. There are major players in Rail logistics in Russia (Takata & Yamanaka 2013), who provide innovative rail transport solutions. They are the specialists for rail-road services within private sector and collaborate with the state railways and roadways for their clients from manufacturing and industrial sector. They would select their carrier as per their customer's business requirement to bring forth optimization in the performance and lower freight charges (Takata & Yamanaka 2013).

They can provide individualized support and render personal touch to their services for the transport needs. Thus, these 3PL Logistics provide rail-road services rendering the rail or road shipping less complex, simple, more efficient and more cost-effective. Their services get aligned with various rail-road logistics initiative which makes their customers' operations more optimized and competitive (Yug Logistics, 2013).

Thus, these companies can manage the outsourced services, together with freight and fleet management as a single-point and convenient service and cost-effective. They can monitor & control the transportation even across and throughout Russian Federation, Turkey, Central Asia, Europe and even other countries (Takata & Yamanaka 2013). This can mean anything and everything to their customer --from tracking, tracing, and managing local or inter-national, to planning & scheduling their consignment (Takata & Yamanaka 2013), to controlling receiving and dispatching. Their Service-Centres provide supportive and information services and manages every aspect of movement of goods service. Thus, they specialize in the provisioning of transport service through private sector haulage (Takata & Yamanaka 2013). This all signifies an even better and efficient transport service which provides the competitive edge to the Logistics giants like "X" (X International Transport Ltd, 2014). Thus, this acts as another major recommendation from this research paper, which would significantly help the companies to mitigate the risks and optimize their logistics processes in the face of the challenge. Especially smaller companies, who cannot afford to maintain their own fleet of transport means, can follow this model rather successfully.

Chapter 5.

In this chapter, mainly from the primary resources and some of the secondary resources, the attempt is made to summarize the challenges posed by the logistics complex of Russia. "Prediction improves the efficiency of logistics since it creates an opportunity for sharing information and resources, not reserves. Perspective techniques and forecast tools today are the methods of stochastic, dynamic and multidimensional prediction based on the identification of relationship between independent and dependent variables as well as economic and mathematical, statistical modelling and simulation" (Fisenko, 2011). In this chapter, the attempt is made to analyse the data as captured from the primary resources like questionnaires and surveys conducted from the company "X" (X International Transport Ltd, 2014). Prediction techniques are used to arrive at the recommendations. Perspective techniques and statistical tools are used for predictions and findings.

5.1 DATA ANALYSIS AND FINDINGS

From the primary resources and some of the secondary resources, in this chapter we will summarize the challenges posed by the logistics complex of Russia. From the survey conducted through the company (X International Transport Ltd, 2014) it is ascertained that it is necessary to resolve and overcome the major challenges and constraints that hamper the development of logistics itself and logistics technologies in Russia, the main ones in researcher's opinion are as follows:

1. Firstly, there is dearth in transport infrastructure which is a pre-requisite for the economic growth and investment activity (Fisenko, 2011) for the national Russian economy. Annual Russian economy losses from bad state of the roads and insufficient level of its development exceed 1.8 trillion ruble or more than 2% of GDP - according to experts it exceeds the government defense spending (also opined by the executives from (X International Transport Ltd, 2014). Poor road infrastructure leads to the fact that the transport component in the cost of production in Russia has reached

20% or more (mostly due to the fact that in Russian exports structure the products of extractive industries have the lion's share and the value of transport costs here is about 50-80% of the commodities prices), whereas in developed countries this figure does not exceed 8% (and for the high-tech products is less than 1-4%)

2. Secondly, in Europe the average rate of commodities movement is 1000 km per day (Fisenko, 2011) while in Russia it is no more than 300 km per day. Finally, the cost of road transportation in Russia is 1.5 times higher than in EU countries (Fisenko, 2011) and the relative fuel consumption is 30% higher than there (X International Transport Ltd, 2014).

It is obvious that the current state of the Russian transport system severely inhibits (Fisenko, 2011) the growth of the national economy. Realizing this the Government intends to significantly increase funding for infrastructure projects. According to the new federal target program for 2010-2015 they are going to allocate 13 trillion ruble (4.7 trillion ruble (Fisenko, 2011) of which are from the federal budget) to the domestic transportation system development. While in 2008 there 300 billion ruble (Fisenko, 2011) of federal funds were allocated for infrastructure development transport investments will grow up to 584 billion ruble in 2010 and up to 770 billion ruble in 2011.

Another Challenge is that because of the irrational development of goods and services (Fisenko, 2011) distribution systems (the absence of a deliberate strategy of distribution systems in industry and commerce, lack of organized commodity markets at large and medium wholesale), inadequate and unstable rates of modern packaging industry development, etc. Despite the fact that the turnover of the packaging market in Russia in 2008 reached 12 billion U.S. dollars and according to the World Packaging Organization (WPO) the Russian packaging market has even entered the top ten largest ones in the world, there are some acute problems in this sector of economy (X International Transport Ltd, 2014).

In 2007 the Russian packaging industry for first time faced with difficulties (Fisenko, 2011) that today can lead to stagnation in the industry. Firstly, some enterprises still have low profitability, (Fisenko, 2011) and secondly, many of the investment programs were suspended or just collapsed. In addition, the sector's infrastructure has reduced its output, but activity of the branch organizations and enterprises including NCPack subcommittee of the Chamber of Commerce and Industry of the Russian Federation (Fisenko, 2011) in development of the packaging industry, as well as the PAKMASH association requires (Fisenko, 2011) further consolidation of opportunities and efforts of above mentioned actors (X International Transport Ltd, 2014). Experts suppose that in 2010 payments delay tendency which started in 2009 will continue its negative impact on profitability of packaging materials production. The production of different types of packaging will be developed unevenly or actually decline (Fisenko, 2011) in production of certain types of packaging may be observed with efforts of raw material industries to increase value of their products while increasing custom taxes for importing resources.

Moreover, it is expected that the influence of raw materials and packaging suppliers from Asia (China and South Korea) will be increased. According to the most pessimistic forecasts,

Problems and Challenges of Russian Transport and Logistics Complex Development turnover of the packaging market in Russia will decline by 10-15% in comparison to previous years.

Another issue is that it includes extremely low level of introducing modern electronic communications systems, electronic networks, communication and telecommunication systems, distribution and transport- logistics centres, informational and computing as well as organizational and legal logistics activities support the low level of industrial-technical base of storage facilities, lack of modern production processing equipment, low level of mechanization and automation of warehouse operations. Distribution system is characterized by the slow advance of goods from producers to consumers, the high level of unmet demand (Fisenko, 2011), unreliable and inadequate quality of service to consumers and insufficient number of freight terminals, as well as their low technical and technological level (X International Transport Ltd, 2014).

Moreover, the issue includes slow pace of modern logistics technologies innovation in transportation and cargo handling such as intermodal, multimodal, and terminal systems, "door-to-door" transportation technology (Fisenko, 2011), advanced telecommunications systems for freight tracking, etc. Today it is not surprise that in recent years logistics companies have more often focused the attention of the economic community. And indeed, their role in the economic life of society is steadily increasing. For example, in 2005 the total turnover (Fisenko, 2011) of the European market of logistics services counted for more than 600 billion euros. Today it is estimated appr. 800-850 billion euros. Approximately 30% of logistics functions (Fisenko, 2011) in all sectors of the economy are handed over to logistics companies every year. Demand for logistics operators is formed by industry and commerce that spend about 120-140 million euros (Fisenko, 2011) annually for the logistics in Europe.

Unfortunately the Russian market for logistics services is not highly developed. Experts estimate its potential as 120 billion U.S. dollars, while the share of cargo forwarding and transportation for all modes of transport is 55%, warehouse services sector figure is 13% (Fisenko, 2011) and integration and supply chain management sector share is 32%. Experts believe that logistics market will be shared by Western companies soon for whom Russia is considered to be the area of interest. International logistics companies from France, Sweden, Germany and other countries operate here. Considering this market development the national operators will need to expand the number of services and improve their quality to meet growing customer requirements to retain their positions. It is possible that some domestic companies will join efforts with international operators.

The Russian logistics market has already had powerful international logistics companies such as "X". There is great interest of major international logistics companies in the Russian warehousing infrastructure driven by the requirements of their international clients. Furthermore, there is an actively developing process of logistics centres and hubs formation in today's Russia, not only within individual modes of transport but also on cross-sectored (Fisenko, 2011) basis, i.e. air-to-rail, rail-to-marine, aviation and railway transport, etc.

Another Challenge is the inefficiency of the Russian customs. Speaking about this critical issue to improve the efficiency of the cargo delivering system it is necessary to radically modify the customs operations, especially at checkpoints. In particular, valuable goods four days delay at the port costs as much as cargo trans-shipping. The existing system of customs clearance reduces the competitiveness of Russian ports. for trans-shipment of high fare container cargo and leads to tangible losses for the operators and the state. Every extra day of downtime adds to the cost of goods up to 0.5% (Fisenko, 2011). Today, the average time for cargo spending on berths in Russia is 35 days, but in the world this figure is just three days. Therefore, many Russian goods are being transported to foreign ports. An impressive example is that according to a survey conducted by DHL the goods transportation cost in Russia is 4 times higher than in China. Another Challenge is the absence of modern means of conveyance that meet world standards almost in all types of transportation as well as high degree of wear and tear of rolling stock equipment.

Thus, we conclude that due to the dearth in

transport infrastructure the Logistics performance index of Russia is very low. The cost of road transportation in Russia is 1.5 times higher than in EU countries. Moreover, there are inadequate and unstable rates of modern packaging industry. The development of modern electronic communications systems, electronic networks, and communication and telecommunication systems develops at an extremely low rate. There is another Challenge: the inefficiency of the Russian customs. Therefore, the Russian Logistics needs to look into these critical issues to improve upon the efficiency of the cargo delivering system. This can be summarized as the challenges posed by the logistics complex of Russia.

Chapter 6.

Conclusions

Thus, we discussed the optimization and the challenges posed by the logistics complex and how the companies tackle the challenges. We also highlighted that the key resources which were utilized to optimize the Logistics complex. In general, the Russian Logistics definitely needs to look into these critical issues to improve upon the efficiency of the cargo delivering system and concentrate to optimize on these processes. The following needs to be looked into to optimize Logistics Processes:

1. As of now there exists an objective demand for the logistics organization of resources provisioning to the national transport sector, as most of the problems, including the issues related with the logistics infrastructure pertains to the dearth of resources.

2. There are challenges of inefficiencies of customs. There is sluggish growth of electronic communication systems. However, meeting-out such challenges in logistics is not possible without proper transport prediction based on a thorough and substantive analysis of the transport industry and related spheres and sectors of national economy. Therefore, it is required that several comprehensive researches be conducted to put forward a thorough and substantive analysis of the transport industry and related spheres and propose the recommendations for improvements.

3. Existing difficulties and problems of the modern state of Transport Logistics Complex in Russia are related with objective and subjective reasons of the previous and the current stage of national development, and can be subdivided into factors of economic, financial, industrial, technological, geographical, political and mental nature. Therefore, to optimize the logistics processes in the face of the challenges, it is extremely necessary to clearly categorize the nature of problems and have a clear understanding of the given logistic concern. Only then one can clearly propose the optimization of the processes in the relevant category.

4. The recommendations and main directions of national Transport Logistics Complex future development are related with:

4.0. the improvement of program-oriented management of the complex,

4.1. development of its logistics and infrastructure, especially improve upon the road logistics

4.2. personnel training and qualification system enhancement, to enhance and improve the logistics operations

4.3. Overall development and search of the

> new forms of international cooperation,
> and explore more active participation
> with successful international players,
> for instance, Company "X".

4.4. Institutional reforms within the
      country aimed at the harmonization
      of "state - society - business"
      relations and create a proper and
      conducive political environment to
      encourage the growth of industries,
      particularly in transport and logistics
      sector

In researcher's opinion, the implementation of the afore-mentioned recommendations in Transport Logistics Complex can catalyze the growth and development of Logistics in Russia. The harmonization of strategic partnership between government, business and society will allow creating conditions for more efficient and competitive integration of Russian economy to the process of increasing consolidation and globalization in transport and logistics services.

As far as the optimization is concerned, the key parameters which help in facing the challenges as posed by the logistics complex and help in minimizing the associated risks, are information, managing resources and outsourcing. With the proper mix and utilization of these resources and parameters and optimally following the recommendations as suggested above, the objectives of overall Logistics optimization is achieved.

Bibliography

Anderson, D.R. et al., 2012. *An Introduction to Management Science: Quantitative Approaches to Decision Making*. 13th ed. South-Western College.

Arlbjorn, J.S. & Halldorsson, A., 2002. *Logistics knowledge creation: reflections on content, context and processes.* International Journal of Physical Distribution & Logistics Management, vol. 32, no. 1 / 2, pp. 22-40.

Armstrong & Associates, 2013. *companies' data*. Armstrong & Associates. https://www.3plogistics.com/.

Armstrong, J.S., ed., 2001. *Principles of Forecasting: A Handbook for Researchers and Practitioners*. Kluwer Academic Publishers.

Armstrong, J.S. & Collopy, F., 1992. Error Measures For Generalizing About Forecasting Methods: Empirical Comparisons. *International Journal of Forecasting*, [Online]. 8(1), pp.69-80. Available at: http://repository.upenn.edu/cgi/viewcontent.cgi?article=1075&context=marketing_papers&sei-redir=1&referer=http%3A%2F%2Fwww.google.co.uk%2Furl%3Fsa%3Dt%26rct%3Dj%26q%3Derror%2520measures%2520for%2520generalizing%2520about%2520forecasting%2520methods%253A%2 [Accessed 2 February 2013].

Armstrong, J.S. & Fildes, R., 1995. On the Selection of Error Measures for Comparisons Among Forecasting Methods. *Journal of Forecasting*, [Online]. 14(1), pp.67-71. Available at:

http://onlinelibrary.wiley.com/doi/10.1002/for.3980140106 /abstract [Accessed 1 February 2013].

Armstrong, J.S. & Lusk, E.J., 1983. The Accuracy of Alternative Extrapolation Models: Analysis of a Forecasting Competition Through Open Peer Review. *Journal of Forecasting*, [Online]. 2(3), pp.259-311. Available at: http://repository.upenn.edu/cgi/viewcontent.cgi?article=1 085&context=marketing_papers [Accessed 24 January 2013].

Asian Institute of Technology in Vietnam, 2013. *Logictics and Supply Chain Management.* http://www.aitvn.asia/en/short-term/100/11565_logictics-and-supply-chain-management.h tml.

Babai, M.Z., Ali, M.M. & Nikolopoulos, K., 2012. Impact of temporal aggregation on stock control performance of intermittent demand estimators: Empirical analysis. *Omega - The International Journal of Management Science*, [Online]. 40(6), pp.713-21. Available at: http://dx.doi.org/10.1016/j.omega.2011.09.004 [Accessed 3 February 2013].

Bolylan, J., Chen, H., Mohammadipour, M. & Syntetos, A., 2013. Formation of seasonal groups and application of seasonal indices. *Journal of the Operational Research Society*, [Online]. pp.1-15. Available at: doi:10.1057/jors.2012.126 [Accessed 16 May 2013].

Bowerman, B.L., O'Connell, R. & Koehler, A.,

2004. *Forecasting, Time series, and*

Regression. Duxbury Press. Brown, R.G.,

1959. *Statistical forecasting for inventory*

control. New York: McGraw-Hill.

Broze, L. & Mélard, G., 1990. Exponential smoothing: Estimation by Maximum Likelihood. *Journal of Forecasting*, [Online]. 9(5), pp.445-55. Available at: doi: 10.1002/for.3980090504 [Accessed 20 April 2013].

Bryman, A. & Bell, E., 2007. *Business Research Methods*. 2nd ed. Oxford University Press.

Buxey, G., 2005. Aggregate planning for seasonal demand: reconciling theory with practice. *International Journal of Operations & Production Management*, [Online]. 25(11), pp.1083-100. Available at: http://dx.doi.org/10.1108/01443570510626907 [Accessed 15 April 2013].

Chang, Y.H., 1998. *Logistical Management*. Hwa-Tai Bookstore Ltd., Taiwan.

Chase, C., 2009. *Demand-Driven Forecasting: A Structured Approach to Forecasting*. John Wiley & Sons.

Chatfield, C., 1978. The Holt-Winters Forecasting Procedure. *Journal of the Royal Statistical Society. Series C (Applied Statistics)*, [Online]. 27(3), pp.264-79. Available at: http://www.jstor.org/stable/2347162 [Accessed 20 January 2013].

Chen, A. & Blue, J., 2010. Performance analysis of demand planning approaches for aggregating, forecasting and disaggregating interrelated demands. *International Journal of Production Economics*, [Online]. 128(2), pp.586-602. Available at: http://dx.doi.org/10.1016/j.ijpe.2010.07.006 [Accessed 03 February 2013].

Chen, I.J. & Paulraj, A., 2004. *Understanding supply chain management: critical research and a theoretical framework*. International Journal of Production Research.

Chiu, H.N., 1995. *The integrated logistics management system: a framework and case study*. Taipei: International Journal of Physical Distribution & Logistics Management,

Vol. 25 No. 6, 1995, pp. 4-22. © MCB University Press, 0960-0035 National Taiwan Institute of Technology, Taipei, Taiwan, Republic of China.

Christopher, M., 2011. *Logistics & Supply Chain Management*. Prentice Hall Financial Times.

Cipra, T. & Hanzak, T., 2011. Exponential Smoothing For TIme Series With Outliers. *Kybernetika*, [Online]. 47, pp.165-78. Available at: http://www.kybernetika.cz/content/2011/2/165/paper.pdf [Accessed 28 January 2013].

Collis, J. & Hussey, R., 2003. *Business Research : A Practical Guide For Undergraduate And Postgraduate Students*. 2nd ed. [Ebook] Palgrave Macmiillan. eBook Collection EBSCOhost.

Collopy, F. & Armstrong, J.S., 1992. Rule-Based Forecasting: Development and Validation of an Expert Systems Approach to Combining Time Series Extrapolations. *Management Science*, [Online]. 38(10), pp.1394-414. Available at: http://www.jstor.org/stable/2632670 [Accessed 27 January 2013].

Daskin, M.S., 1992. *Logistics: an overview of the state of the art and perspectives on future research*. Transportation Research, Vol. 19A Nos 5/6, 1985, pp. 383-98..

Dawson, C., 2002. *Practical Research Methods: A User-friendly Guide to Mastering Research Techniques and Projects*. 1st ed. How to Books Ltd.

Dekker, M., Donselaar, K.v. & Ouwehand, P., 2004. How to use aggregation and combined forecasting to improve seasonal demand forecasts. *International Journal of Production Economics*, [Online]. 90(2), pp.151-67. Available at: http://dx.doi.org/10.1016/j.ijpe.2004.02.004 [Accessed 2 February 2013].

Efimova, E.G. & Tsenzharik, M.K., 2009. *Electronic Logistics Services in Russia: the bridge to United Europe*. Electronic Publications of Pan-European Institute 3/2009.

Farnum, N.R., 1992. Exponential Smoothing: Behavior of the Ex-Post Sum of Squares near 0 and 1. *Journal of Forecasting*, [Online]. 11(1), p.47. Available at: http://search.proquest.com/docview/219159544?accountid=7179 [Accessed 10 April 2013].

Fisenko, A.I., 2011. *STATUS, PROBLEMS AND CHALLENGES OF RUSSIAN TRANSPORT AND LOGISTICS COMPLEX DEVELOPMENT*.
Asia-Pacific Journal of Marine Science&Education, Vol. 1, No. 1, 2011, pp. 31-42.

Frechtling, D.C., 2001. *Forecasting Tourism Demand: Methods and Strategies*. 1st ed. Butterworth-Heinemann.

Gardner, E.S., 1985. Exponential Smoothing: The State of the Art. *Journal of Forecasting*, [Online]. 4(1), pp.1-28. Available at: EBSCOHost [Accessed 25 January 2013].

Gardner, E.S. & McKenzie, E., 1988. Model Identification in Exponential Smoothing. *The Journal of the Operational Research Society*, [Online]. 39(9), pp.863-67. Available at: http://www.jstor.org/stable/2583529 [Accessed 22 January 2013].

Gelper, S., Fried, R. & Croux, C., 2007. *Robust Forecasting with Exponential and Holt-Winters Smoothing*. [Online] Available at: https://lirias.kuleuven.be/bitstream/123456789/120456/1/K BI_0718.pdf [Accessed 21 February 2013].

Handfield, R., Straube, F., Pfohl, H.-C. & Wieland, A., 2013.

Embracing Global Logistics Complexity to Drive Market Advantage. DVV Media Group GmbH.

Harrison, A. & van Hoek, R., 2008. *Logistics Management and Strategy: Competing through the supply chain*. Pearson Education.Chicago.

Harvard, n.d. *Research Methods: Some Notes to Orient You*. [Online] Available at: http://isites.harvard.edu/fs/docs/icb.topic851950.files/Research%20Methods_Some%20Notes.pdf [Accessed 27 January 2013].

Holmström, J., Ala-Risku, T., Främling, K. & Kärkkäinen, M., 2008. *Evaluating Research-in-process: At The Cutting Edge Of Solution Design And Supply Chain Management Theory*. Helsinki University of Technology.

Hyndman, R.J. & Koehler, A.B., 2006. Another look at measures of forecast accuracy. *International Journal of Forecasting*, [Online]. 22(4), pp.679-6888. Available at: http://dx.doi.org/10.1016/j.ijforecast.2006.03.001 [Accessed 31 January 2013].

Hyndman, R., Makridakis, S.G. & Wheelwright, S.C., 1998. *Forecasting: Methods and Applications*. 3rd ed. John Wiley & Sons Inc.

intel, 2003. *Automatic identification*. Intel.

ITS Russia, 2013. *ITS Networking*. http://www.itsnetwork.org/en/members/its_russia.htm.

Jain, C.L., 2006. Benchmarking Forecasting Errors. *Journal of Business Forecasting*, 25(18), p.18. [Accessed 27 April 2013].

Kim, S., Cohen, M.A. & Netessine, S., 2006. *Performance Contracting in After-Sales Service Supply Chains*. Philadelphia: http://knowledge.wpengine.com/wp-content/uploads/2013/09/1334.pdf The Wharton School, University of Pennsylvania.

KORECKÝ, M., 2012. *RISK MANAGEMENT IN LOGISTICS*. Carpathian Logistics congress.

Kumar, S.A. & Suresh, N., 2008. *Production and Operations Management*. 2nd ed. [eBook] New Age Publishers. Available at: http://tn.upi.edu/pdf/Production_and_Operations_Management.pdf [accessed 5 February 2013].

LambertD., D.M. & Stock, J.R., 1993. *Strategic Logistics Management*. 3rd ed., Richard D. Irwin, Homewood, IL, 1993, p. 4.

Maddala, G.S. & Kim, I.-M., 1999. *Unit Roots, Cointegration, and Structural Change*. Reprinted ed. Cambridge University Press.

Makridakis, S. & Hibon, M., 2000. The M3-Competition: results, conclusions and implications. *International Journal of Forecasting*, [Online]. 16(4), pp.451-76. Available at: http://dx.doi.org/10.1016/S0169-2070(00)00057-1 [Accessed 2 February 2013].

Makridakis, S.G. & Wheelwright, S.C., 1977. *Forecasting Methods for Management*. Wiley.

Matthiassen, 2002. *ollaborative practice research*. Information Technology & People, vol. 15, no. 4, pp. 321-345.

Meredith, J., 1998. *Building operations management theory through case and field research*. Journal of Operations Management, vol. 16, no. 4, pp. 441-454..

Muth, J.F., 1960. Optimal Properties of Exponentially Weighted Forecasts. *Journal of the American Statistical Association*, [Online]. 55, pp.299-306. Available at: http://www.jstor.org/stable/2281742 [Accessed 25 January 2013].

National Credit Bureau, 2010. *Companies' data*. Ros Business Consulting.

Nikolopoulos, K. et al., 2011. An aggregate–disaggregate intermittent demand approach (ADIDA) to forecasting: an empirical proposition and analysis. *Journal of the Operational Research Society*, [Online]. 62(3), pp.544-54. Available at: http://dx.doi.org/10.1057/jors.2010.32 [Accessed 03 February 2013].

Ohmae, K., 1983. *The Mind of the Strategist*. Penguin Books, 1983.

Ord, K., 2004. Charles Holt's report on exponentially weighted moving averages: an introduction and appreciation. *International Journal of Forecasting*, [Online]. 20(1), pp.1-3. Available at: http://dx.doi.org/10.1016/j.ijforecast.2003.09.016 [Accessed 3 February 2013].

Pickering, A., 1995. *"The Mangle of Practice: Time, Agency & Science"*. hicago University Press.

Pindyck, R.S. & Rubinfeld, D.L., 1998.

Econometric Models and Economic

Forecasts. Singapore: Irwin McGraw-Hill.

Posternakova, M., 2012. *Benchmarking*.

http://www.russiasupplychain.com/benchm

arking-in-the-cis/.

PWC, 2013. *Transportation and Logistics:V olume 3: Emerging Markets – New hubs, new spokes, new industry leaders?*

PricewaterhouseCoopers.

Ragsdale, C.T., 2008. *Managerial Decision Modeling*. International ed. ed. South Western College.
Reck, R.F. & Long, B.G., 1988. *Purchasing a competitve Weapon*. Journal of Purchasing and MAterials Management. RosBusinessConsulting, 2011. *RUSSIAN TRANSPORT AND LOGISTICS SERVICES MARKET IN 2010-2011 AND FORECAST TO 2014.*

Moscow: RBC Research Ros business consulting.

Roslow, S., Li, T. & Nicholls, J.A.F., 2000. Impact of situational variables and demographic attributes in two seasons on purchase behaviour. *European Journal of Marketing*, [Online]. 34(9/10), pp.1167-80. Available at: http://dx.doi.org/10.1108/03090560010342548 [Accessed 7 April 2013].

Rushton, A., Croucher, P. & Baker, P., 2010. *The Handbook of Logistics and Distribution Management*. Kogan Page Publishers. Saunders, T., Lewis, P. & Thornhill, A., 2007.

Research Methods for Business Students. Pearson Education.

Savi, 2003. *Automatic identification*. Savi.

Sbrana, G. & Silvestrini, A., 2010. *Aggregation of Exponential Smoothing Processes with an Application to Portforlio Risk Evaluation*. [Online] Available at: http://www.uclouvain.be/cps/ucl/doc/core/documents/cor edp2010_39web.pdf [Accessed 2 February 2013].

Simon, H., 1996. *The Sciences of the Artificial*. The MIT Press, Cambridge, Mass., USA, 3rd Edition, pp. 231.

Spekman, R.E., Kamauff Jr, J.W. & Myhr, N., 1998. *An empirical investigation into supply chain management*. Supply Chain Management, Vol. 3 No. 2, 1998.

Stevenson, W.J., 2011. *Operations Management*. 11th ed. McGraw-Hill Higher Education.

Stock, G.N., Greis, N.P. & Kasarda, J.D., 2000.

Enterprise logistics. Journal of Operations

Management. Summers, M.R., 1998.

Analyzing Operations in Business: Issues,

Tools, and Techniques. 1st ed. Praeger.

Tabar, B.R., Ducq, Y., Babai, M.Z. & Syntetos, A.A., 2012. *Forecasting Autoregressive Demands with Temporal Aggregation*. [Online] Available at: http://hal.archives-ouvertes.fr/docs/00/72/85/74/PDF/paper _196.pdf [Accessed 3 February 2013].

Tratar, L.F., 2010. Joint optimisation of demand forecasting and stock control parameters. *International Journal of Production Economics*, [Online]. 127(1), pp.173-79. Available at: http://dx.doi.org/10.1016/j.ijpe.2010.05.009 [Accessed 20 January 2013].

TSENG, Y., TAYLOR, M.A.P. & YUE, W.L., 2005. *THE ROLE OF TRANSPORTATION IN LOGISTICS CHAIN*. roceedings of the Eastern

Asia Society for Transportation Studies, Vol. 5, pp. 1657 - 1672, 2005.

Tuominen, P.M., 2009. *ST. PETERSBURG – A LOGISTICS PERSPECTIVE*. T A M P E R E 2 0 0 9.

Weele, A.V., 2002. *Purchasing and Supply Chain*

Management. Analysis Planning and Practice 3rd

edition, Thomson. Wim Bosman Russia, 2013. *Wim*

Bosman enhances logistics planning and analysis with assino support. Wim Bosman. World Bank Report, 2014. *Connecting to Compete 2014 Trade Logistics in the Global Economy*. World Bank Report.

Yug Logistics, 2013. *innovative Rail Transport Solutions*. http://www.yuglog.com/dosya/yuglog_brosur.pdf.

Zotteri, G., Kalchschmidt, M. & Caniato, F., 2005. The impact of aggregation level on forecasting performance. *International Journal of Production Economics*, [Online]. 93-94, pp.479-91. Available at: http://dx.doi.org/10.1016/j.ijpe.2004.06.044 [Accessed 3 February 2013].

Appendix

Questionnaire

1. Please rank these items from 1 to 7 in order of importance to you. (1 being the most important):
2. How many carriers do you currently manage?

   1 - 3
   4 - 9
   10 - 20
    12 or More

3. How many points of contact do you currently need to manage?

   1 - 3
   4 - 9
   11 - 20 12 or More

5. Please provide the below Annual shipping Metrics:
   |

   ,
   What is your annual freight spend ?
5. Do you currently audit your freight bills?

6. How many hours do you annually spend in the following areas? Load planning Rate shopping Shipment tracking
   Freight bill reconciliation

9. Please rate the following points for newly developed logistics area (1=least, 5=most important)

a) Have sufficient space for lorry parking and waiting
b) Access to high speed road system
c) Railway link for high-volume and low cost transport
d) Near to Sea or River terminal
e) Food catering and resting facilities
f) Far away from residential areas
g) Others, please specify

10. Do you plan to outsource logistics service providers other than mentioned at the site? If so, please state their names.
11. Which of the following logistics services do you want to outsource to a logistics service provider?

12. Are your products stored at a special rehouse before shipping? Yes/No

13. What % of the total
    annual volume pass
    through the warehouse?
    (Versus going directly
    from factory to client.)

14. How much warehousing space do you
    need?

15. Is there any special storage
    arrangement required? If yes please
    specify

16. Order handling: What are the Order
    quantities? (Average number of orders
    per month)

17. Do you expect to have rush orders?
    Yes/No

18. What is the Normal delivery lead time
    ?(from order entry until delivery)

(This will help in operational efficiency an
object of research)

19. Do you expect express shipments?

(This will help in operational efficiency an
object of research)